A PORTFOLIO OF

BEDROOM
IDEAS

CONTENTS

A Portfolio of Bedroom Ideas cont.

© Copyright 1995
Cy DeCosse Incorporated
5900 Green Oak Drive
Minnetonka, Minnesota 55343
1-800-328-3895
All rights reserved

Printed in Hong Kong
Library of Congress
Cataloging-in-Publication Data
Portfolio of Flooring Ideas
p. cm.

ISBN 0-86573-962-5 (softcover)
1. Bedrooms. 2. Interior decoration.
I. Cy DeCosse Incorporated.
NK2117.B4P67 1995
747.7'7—dc20
95-21129
CIP

Author: Home How-To Institute™
Creative Director: William B. Jones
Associate Creative Director: Tim Himsel
Project Director: Paul Currie
Managing Editor: Carol Harvatin
Art Directors: Gina Seeling, Ruth Eischens, Geoff Kinsey
Copy Editor: Janice Cauley
Technical Artist: Jon Simpson
Vice President of Development
   Planning & Production: Jim Bindas
Production Manager: Linda Halls

Printed by: Shiny International (1195)

CY DECOSSE INCORPORATED

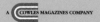
A COWLES MAGAZINES COMPANY

Chairman/CEO: Bruce Barnet
Chairman Emeritus: Cy DeCosse
President & Chief Operating Officer: Nino Tarantino
Editor-in-Chief: William B. Jones

The latest designs in modular storage offer innovative new ways to help you organize and make the most of your bedroom space.

A spacious master bedroom has enough room to include a reading niche with a luxurious lounger next to the window.

Futon couches that convert to beds are ideal for one-room studio apartments and spare rooms that sometimes double as sleeping quarters.

WHAT MAKES A GREAT BEDROOM?

Of any room in a house, the bedroom is the most intimate. More than a resting place, a bedroom is a personal sanctuary where you can escape to enjoy complete privacy. Bedrooms today reflect the many ways the use of this personal space has evolved and expanded. Today's bedrooms are state-of-the-art, multiuse living areas that include home offices, home theaters, workout areas, even art collections.

Whether you're planning to redo a master bedroom, create a comfortable guest room or update a chaotic kids' space, *A Portfolio of Bedroom Ideas* explores a variety of options that are sure to inspire you. You'll discover master

suites that are all-inclusive retreats complete with spa and exercise area. Explore innovative new ideas for bedroom storage, including space-saving built-in units. Find ways to create colorful kids' rooms that are durable, flexible and easily adaptable to children's changing needs for space. You'll also find helpful planning and decorating hints as well as tips for choosing accessories such as furniture, mattresses, bedding and window treatments.

The second half of the book is a portfolio section that showcases a variety of beautiful bedrooms, ranging in style from Victorian to contemporary.

ASSESSING YOUR NEEDS

Begin by assessing your existing bedroom. What needs are being met, and what is lacking? What do you like or dislike? Do you want more morning light? More storage space? Have your space needs changed? Have the kids moved out so you have extra space? Or have you added to your family, creating new space needs?

If you're starting from scratch your options are wide open; you have the luxury of choosing the size and location, even the layout of your bedroom. On the other hand, if you're dealing with a bedroom that already exists, there is a good chance you will be limited by space and layout restrictions. Although your options may seem limited, there are more alternatives to choose from than one might think.

Because bedrooms are such personal rooms, not usually seen by many outsiders, they often evolve into one of the most eclectic rooms in the house. A bedroom is often the place where you'll find collections of personal art and memorabilia, photographs, even a favorite piece of furniture, all tied together into one harmonious look—sometimes depicting a specific style, sometimes just an overall feel or theme. Decorative elements such as style, color, pattern and texture will also play a part in the final look you create.

Often we are limited by budget constraints when remodeling. There are a number of simple improvements that can be made in a bedroom that don't cost a lot, and will achieve very effective results. Altering the floor plan and redefining the space can make what you already have more usable and efficient. If structural changes aren't possible at this time, easy updates like replacing old wallpaper, adding recessed lights or installing plush new carpet can breathe new life into an old bedroom. This type of remodel won't solve any space constriction problems, but the changes are easy and can do almost as much for the look of a bedroom as rearranging the walls—at half the cost.

A structural change is the most effective way to make a dramatic difference in an existing bedroom. A new bay window or a walk-in closet can change the entire feel of the room.

***Give the nursery** a quaint touch of country with a hand-crafted wooden cradle.*

Photo courtesy of Cy DeCosse Inc.

(above) **Double French doors** are used to subtly separate this master bedroom from the adjacent bath. When the doors are ajar, the opening visually enlarges the sense of space and links the two rooms; when closed, the room become a more intimate and private space.

(left) **A cozy play area** is tucked into the corner of a children's room. This busy area has all of the essentials: a low table for coloring, built-in shelves for storage and a big soft chair for snuggling while listening to bedtime stories.

DESIGNING A FLOOR PLAN

If you could design the ideal bedroom, it would be large enough to hold whatever size bed you desire, with ample room for furniture and accessories. Unfortunately, many times the case is just the opposite; once the bed is chosen and in place, you're faced with trying to fit everything else into the remaining space without overcrowding.

Taking time to plan can help you to foresee any possible space usage problems. Begin by surveying your existing bedroom, then analyze your options for improvement. Study the layout of the space and think about how it can work best for you. A good design is practical and comfortable, as well as stylish.

Because the bed is usually the largest item in the room, its location is critical to making the most effective use of the space. Traffic patterns begin and end at the bed. The location of other areas, such as a dressing or sitting area, will then evolve from the bed's placement. Start experimenting with your floor plan options by trying various furniture arrangements on paper instead of trying to push heavy furniture around the room.

Try to imagine being in your bedroom with the type of bed you want, placed where you think it works best. Does this new floor plan make the most efficient use of floor space?

Think about what you will see from the bed. Will morning light waken you or glare into your eyes? Allow enough clearance in places where a door swings inward or a drawer pulls open. Be sure to allow enough clearance above the bed as well, especially with a platform bed. Four feet of headroom is the minimum that should be allotted.

To create the illusion of a larger space, avoid clutter. Keep as much floor area open as possible. Placing the bed in a corner is one way to make the rest of the floor area seem larger. A studio apartment or a small bedroom can double as a sitting room by using a sofa bed, futon couch or daybed (a bed with two ends) rather than a conventional bed.

The guidelines for bedroom furniture arrangements are more flexible because these rooms don't have as much traffic as other rooms. These guidelines allow you to use some tricks to help make a bedroom more useful. Beds can be free-standing, positioned with one end or side against the wall, angled into the room, or tucked into a corner or a special niche. If you're dealing with limited floor space or a seldom-used guest room, a loft bed, bunk bed, Murphy bed, trundle or other built-in may be the answer.

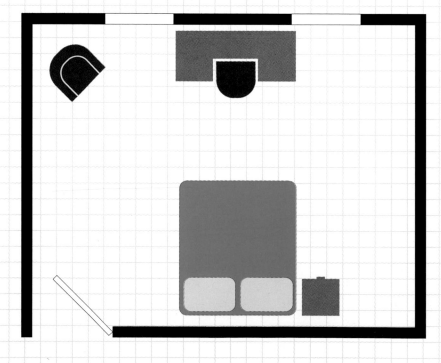

*To **help you experiment** with different floor plan options, draw your room to scale on grid paper—be sure to include any door openings and windows. Then cut paper pieces to scale representing the various elements of the room: a bed, dresser, chair, etc. You can now rearrange these elements to determine the configuration that works best.*

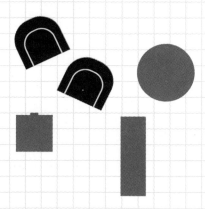

Floor space is *optimized* *by incorporating built-in elements as much as possible. Integrated shelving and storage systems give you maximum efficiency.*

The diagonal direction *of the hardwood flooring helps this bedroom seem larger than it actually is. The furniture arrangement creates a natural pathway to the dressing area just through the doorway.*

Planning
STORAGE

Don't forget to include your bedroom storage needs when assessing your current space. Begin by taking inventory of what needs to be stored, and where. Create additional bedroom storage by moving seasonal clothing to another part of the house, such as a basement or spare room. Once you have decided what you want stored in the bedroom, you can begin creating a storage system that best accommodates your needs.

Most bedrooms include one of two types of closets: a walk-in (a closet deep enough to walk into, with room for storage on either side) or a wall closet. Wall closets are not as deep, and run along the wall. The American Institute of Architects has established some basic guidelines for standard closet measurements. These measurements are based on the general dimensions of clothing and can be used in any type of closet to help you decide where to hang shelves, closet rods and other hardware.

Remember to take advantage of the space above closet poles and any unused space under the bed to create new storage areas. Modular storage is an ideal option for bedrooms. It conserves valuable floor space and is cost effective. You can create a system piece by piece, at your own pace, purchasing sections as your budget allows. If storage space in your bedroom is limited, some bed frames, such as platforms and waterbeds, often have built-in storage compartments.

(right) **Uncluttered contemporary** *is the look of this luxurious bedroom. A combination of integrated shelves, drawers and hanging storage keeps everything organized and out of sight. (below)* **A place for everything,** *and everything in its place is the idea behind this all-inclusive closet system.*

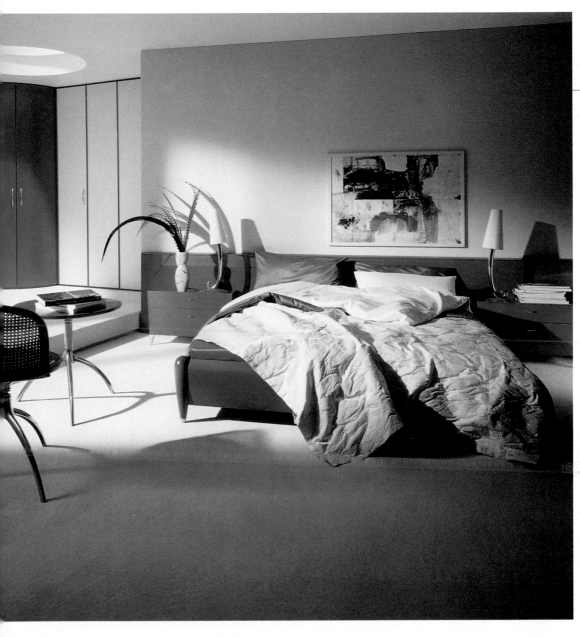

Make every inch count by installing closet hardware and accessories to carefully measured proportions. Shelves, pull-out bins and other components can be assembled to suit your specific storage needs.

photos both pages courtesy of Interlubke, North America

Hats 6"

Full length 68"

Sweaters & Folded Shirts 14"

Misc. storage 9"

Suits & Shirts 38"

Misc. storage length varies

There are many different types of ready-made storage units available to help you organize your storage space most efficiently. Modular storage units for your bedroom come in different design styles, from ultracontemporary, high-tech European design, to stackable plastic bins. This type of storage offers affordable flexibility for future storage needs. You can rearrange and add pieces as your needs change.

When choosing a modular unit, look at the quality of the construction throughout the entire unit. Look for drawers that have sturdy corners and open smoothly with center or side guides.

Storage needs vary from room to room, even from one kind of bedroom to another. Bedrooms that are multifunctional, such as a guest room that also serves as a sewing center, may have special storage needs. In children's rooms, storage needs are more diverse; items such as toys, books, clothes and more all need to find a convenient home.

An ultramodern modular system includes specialty storage features for optimal closet organization. (top left) **Flat storage** *keeps shirts wrinkle-free and ready whenever you are. (bottom left)* **Collapsable canvas bags** *act as hanging hampers for delicate dry cleanables.*

(top right) **Swinging tie rack** *turns out to display wares, then turns back into the closet.*
(bottom right) **See-through drawer ends** *provide you with a convenient view of what's inside.*

*This **swing-arm lamp** puts eye comfort first. A wall-mounted version of this lovely lamp style can be adjusted, as needed, to meet your nighttime reading needs.*

Photo courtesy of Casella Lighting

Design

LIGHTING

Lighting in a bedroom plays an important part in creating the environment you desire. Creative lighting is the most flexible and effective way to change the mood or ambience of a room. The entire look of a room can be lost if proper consideration is not given to the lighting. It is important to realize that light is a medium that can be manipulated, changed and directed for different effects. When searching for lighting ideas, look at the effect the light will achieve, as well as the appearance of the light itself.

There are three types of lighting: background, or ambient, lighting, which provides general light throughout the entire room; task lighting, to read or work by; and accent, or spot, lighting, to highlight special features.

Bedroom lighting needs to meet a variety of criteria; it must be soft enough to be relaxing and peaceful, yet bright enough to allow you to see when dressing. The location of lighting in the bedroom is as important as the light fixture itself. Bedside lamps should be at a height where they shine directly onto a book. Lights located at either side of a makeup mirror are better than lights that shine from above or behind. The same applies to full-length mirrors—the light should be directed onto the the viewer or the subject, preferably from the side.

Natural light will also have a different effect on the look of a room. Skylights and large windows are one way to let in more light. After sundown the look of a bedroom can change dramatically, creating a need for various types of artificial lighting.

There should be a fixture or switch that can be easily accessed from the bed. To make sure they are installed in a location that is comfortably accessible, you may want to sit in the bed while deciding where to install lights and switches. Light fixtures should be located behind anyone reading, so the light falls over a shoulder. If the light is coming from an overhead source, it should fall one foot in front of the work or book; otherwise, the illumination will be too bright. The most effective bedroom lighting layout includes swing-arm lamps with integral dimmers located at the appropriate height.

Color and design will also influence what happens to light in a bedroom. By manipulating all of these elements correctly, you can create a balance of light and shade that has a spectacular effect on a room.

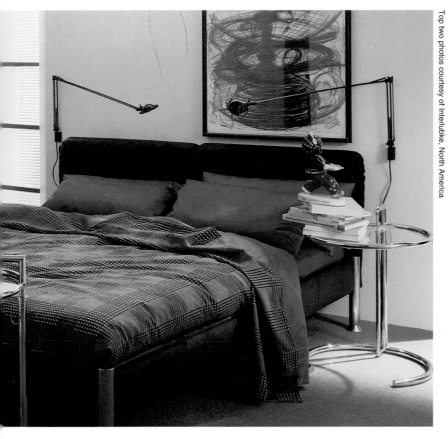

Top two photos courtesy of Interlubke, North America

(above) **Ultramodern adjustable table lamp** adjusts to any position or reading level and has a sleek, sturdy base for stability and balance.

(left) **Matching swing-arm lamps** are mounted on the wall where they are out of the way, yet easily accessed.

(left) **The custom lighting** in this bedroom includes recessed lights, installed in an overhead soffit. A dimmer switch is located close to the bed, for adjusting this general lighting. Table lamps sit bedside to direct light onto the reading material. Both are easily accessed from the comfort of the bed.

Photo courtesy of Cy DeCosse Inc.

Design
COLOR, PATTERN & TEXTURE

Color is one of the key elements in a bedroom's decor. When redecorating your bedroom, use items you already have—a rug, a painting, a bedspread or bed frame—as a starting point for your color scheme.

Light is an important factor to consider when choosing a color scheme for a bedroom. The type of light, natural or artificial, will affect the way a color looks in a room. The colors you use, warm or cool, subtle or intense,

will affect the entire mood or ambience of the setting. Colors also influence the perceived size of a room. A bedroom that doesn't receive much sunlight during the day will seem bigger and brighter if you make it as light as possible. Light colors tend to make a space appear larger than it really is. Conversely, dark colors make a space seem smaller. A high ceiling or walls can be painted a darker or deeper color to make a bedroom feel more intimate.

Tapestry fabrics, with rich colors and interesting textures, can be used to create decorative wall hangings, throws or area rugs.

A bedroom with a view. *The colors and textures of the scenery outside are imitated in the delicate floral patterns used throughout. The curtains, upholstery, even the wallpaper, have all been planned to beautifully coordinate the look of this interior.*

17

When selecting a color scheme for your bedroom, let personal taste guide you rather than current trends. If the bedroom is predominantly one color, vary the textures to add interest; for example, combine a smooth, crisp chintz fabric with a textured linen.

Keep in mind that walls, floors and other elements in a bedroom also have textures that add to the ambience of a room. A smooth brass headboard contrasts nicely with a tapestry bedspread. Polished hardwood flooring provides a beautiful surface that sets off a plush area rug perfectly. Effectively combining patterns to create a desired bedroom decor can be a bit confusing and somewhat intimidating. Today, many textile manufacturers are making things easier for their customers by offering such coordinating elements as fabric and wallpaper together, to make the whole process easier.

One way to successfully combine patterns is to use one fairly large design and contrast it with a geometric pattern, such as stripes, a plaid, checks or even polka dots. The patterns should coordinate with each other through color or tone with subtle contrasts of scale or proportion. It is best not to use more than one large-scale design in a room. Try using several different small-scale patterns with a larger design.

Deep colors and bold patterns are used in this grand bedroom to visually draw the room closer together. Rich orange walls and a hunter green area rug combine, in an effective use of color, to draw this expansive bedroom space closer together.

Photo courtesy of Grange

Flowers from floor to ceiling. This bedroom is awash in a floral pattern that covers the walls and drapes around the windows. Even the chair is covered in matching material.

Patterns are incorporated into design schemes in a few different ways. One way is to use plain, unpatterned walls, windows and furnishings with muted colors to keep the look simple. A Shaker motif would be one example. Another approach is to use pattern throughout, on the windows, the walls, even on the furnishings.

When mixing patterns in a bedroom, use only one bold pattern throughout so that it dominates the design. You can then begin adding smaller-scale patterns and prints. A third choice is to use patterns with plain color together for a balanced look. A larger pattern on a window treatment or walls gives the room a sense of balance if other items in the room, such as the blinds, upholstery, pillows or cushions, are kept as simple as possible.

Similar designs in the same colors work well together, as do similar designs in two different colors. An exception to the rule of not using too many patterns together can be made with patterns that have similar color and scale of design, such as plaids or paisleys.

A rainbow of color is used to create a setting that is both bold and beautiful. The muted tones of the wall and floor create a background that visually ties the room together and anchors the vivid accent colors.

Photos both pages courtesy of Interlubke, North America

20

The vibrant colors in this bedroom setting are intensified by the bright, clean white walls and window treatments.

Design
BEDDING

The way a bed is dressed can establish the character of the entire room. An easy way to change your bedroom is simply to change the bedding. Creating a beautiful bed is easier today than ever before; practically everything you could possibly need is available in color-coordinated designer collections.

Many bedding collections feature sheets, bedspreads, duvet or comforter covers, bed skirts and pillows in all types of coordinating patterns, solids, stripes or plaids. Matching fabrics for window blinds, valances, bed skirts, canopies, pillow cases and cushions, as well as wallpapers and borders, are also available. These coordinating accessories make it possible to give your bedroom a whole new look without spending a lot.

New designer sheets alone can be used any number of ways to achieve a desired style when decorating a bedroom. The highest-quality and most expensive bed sheets are made of linen. It doesn't soil as easily and doesn't retain moisture as much as cotton does. This cool, smooth material is especially comfortable in summer. Today, color-coordinated designer bedding is made of linen, cotton and other blends.

Beautiful bedding makes the bed. Cool, comfortable cotton bedding feels good and looks great, even when it's a little ruffled.

Photo courtesy of Cy DeCosse Inc.

(top left) **Bright new ideas in bedding** can help you bring an old-fashioned country style to your bedroom. Bedding ensembles offer a coordinated version of almost every bedding item available—and then some, if you count the matching material that is often available for these sets. If you can create it, you can coordinate with your bedroom.

(top right) **A clever kids' space** uses brightly colored gingham to unite the room in a cheery, checked decor. Simple cotton sheets were used to create the coordinated bedding accessories.

Customized bedding items are also available. Tailored bed skirts feature pleats at the corners and at the center of each side.

Pillow covers, shams and cases add a decorative flair to a bed. They can create a look that's trimmed and tailored, or fluffy and frilly. Bedspreads, quilts and duvets, or comforters, dress a bed in very different ways. Specialty sheets, such as satin or flannel, can be found in the linen departments. Sheets for specially shaped beds, such as round or heart-shaped, can be custom-ordered.

The bedspread was established by wealthy Americans who felt a properly made bed always included the blanket cover and the quilted bedspread that hid the bedclothes. The quilt evolved from the early American settlers. When the bedding they brought from Europe started to wear and fray, they would cut pieces of torn garments and patch it. Traditional American quilts have three layers; the top design, the batting or lining, and the backing.

Bed pillows vary in size depending on the amount of stuffing used. Measure the pillow to determine the size of pillow sham or case you will need.

Photo courtesy of Cy DeCosse Inc.

The covered look of a canopy bed was the inspiration for this downscaled version. The effect was created by draping a swag of matching material from the ceiling.

Two bottom photos courtesy of Laura Ashley

Periwinkle blue is picked up in all of the bedding elements, from the duvet to the pillow covers, to tie this pretty bedroom setting together perfectly.

Popular bedding coordinates have expanded to include matching window treatments and wallpapers, as well as other bedding accessories such as the pillow and duvet covers. Even the window seat has been upholstered in a matching material.

Design
WINDOW
TREATMENTS

The primary function of a window treatment in a bedroom is to control light and provide privacy. The type of treatment you choose will affect how well you can control these elements, as well as influence the decorative style of the room.

Open-weave curtains and blinds bring a breezy, casual feeling to a room, while thick, elegant draperies and fancy top treatments, such as valances or cornices, have a formal influence in a bedroom.

The type of fabric or material, and style of curtain or drapery, will influence the overall effect of a window treatment on the room's design. Sheer curtains filter light and provide privacy during the daylight, but they need a heavier curtain behind them at night to maintain this privacy.

*The **right window** treatment can make a world of difference; it can transform an ordinary window into a work of art.*

Photo courtesy of Cy DeCosse Inc.

(bottom) **Creative use of simple window treatments** like the sheer curtains used here, helps visually increase the sense of space in a smaller bedroom. Lightweight, translucent curtains lightly draped from one corner to the other create an effect that fits the interesting tropical motif.

(left) **Custom-fit vertical blinds** are not only an effective way to control and direct light through this triangular window; they also create a dramatic visual effect when backlit by sunlight.

*The **delicate material** of these curtains creates a look that is light and lacy. The sheer material lets in lots of sunlight during the day, but needs something opaque behind it at night to provide privacy.*

WINDOW TREATMENTS

Curtains are the most common and versatile type of window treatment used today. Many curtains that seem complicated and elaborate are simply variations of the common rod-pocket curtain. The looks that can be achieved by varying this style of curtain range from bishop sleeves to cafe curtains and valances.

Blinds, shades and shutters are also window treatment options for a bedroom. Blinds come in vertical and horizontal styles and an array of colors, sizes and materials. Louvered blinds can be opened or closed to let in light as desired.

Shades provide privacy, block light and conserve energy. Popular shade styles include: Austrian shades, which draw up into scalloped folds; Roman shades, which form neat horizontal folds; balloon shades, which form billows; and cloud shades, which create soft, cloudlike poufs.

Or combine curtains and draperies with coordinating blinds or shades to establish an entirely new look for a window.

*(top right) **A simple Roman shade** of woven material keeps the look casual and uncluttered.*

*(top left) **Billowy balloon shades** in matching material complement the flowery, ruffled motif of this bedroom beautifully.*

*(below) **A deep maroon satin valance**, with silky tassels, adds a touch of old-fashioned elegance to a traditional look.*

Design
CHOOSING A BED

The natural focal point of the bedroom is the bed itself; this means the selection of the bed is important in establishing the overall design of a bedroom, particularly if the frame is unusually interesting. The variety of bed styles available ranges from a simple futon mat, to a traditional box spring and mattress, to a waveless waterbed, with variations and alternatives in between.

In the United States, standard sizes were established in the 1950s for bed frames and mattresses: King, 72" x 84"; Queen, 60" x 75"; double or full, 54" x 52"; and single or twin, 39" x 75". Unless your bed is older than this, it will be one of these universal sizes, regardless of the type of bed frame. And although the sizes of American beds and bedding were standardized in the 1950s, the closest-to-standard sizes in pillows include: king, 26" x 36"; queen, 26" x 30" and standard, 20" x 26". Other pillow sizes include French continental or eurosquare, 26" x 26" and the Russian pillow, 14" x 14".

Futons are ideal for studios and small spaces, as are Murphy beds. First introduced in 1905, the Murphy bed folds into a closet to open up more floor space when not in use. Some are hinged at the head and some hinge at the side.

Bunk beds and trundle bed styles are space-saving alternatives to an extra bed in the guest room. Bunk beds are stacked on top of one another, while trundle beds have a second bed that slides out from underneath the first bed. Bunk beds are primarily found in children's rooms.

Covered buttons and padded upholstery were used to create this custom headboard. The upholstered look of the headboard gives the bedroom setting a softer feel.

Photo Courtesy of Cy DeCosse Inc.

*A **simple futon*** *can be very versatile—folded up it makes a comfortable couch—easily opened, it converts to a bed.*

To make maximum use *of minimal floor space, a bed that folds out from a built-in cabinet, similar to a Murphy-style bed, is integrated into a modular bedroom system.*

*A **daybed,*** *distinguished by headboards at both ends, becomes a cozy niche for reading or relaxing, when covered with soft, cushy pillows and a comforter.*

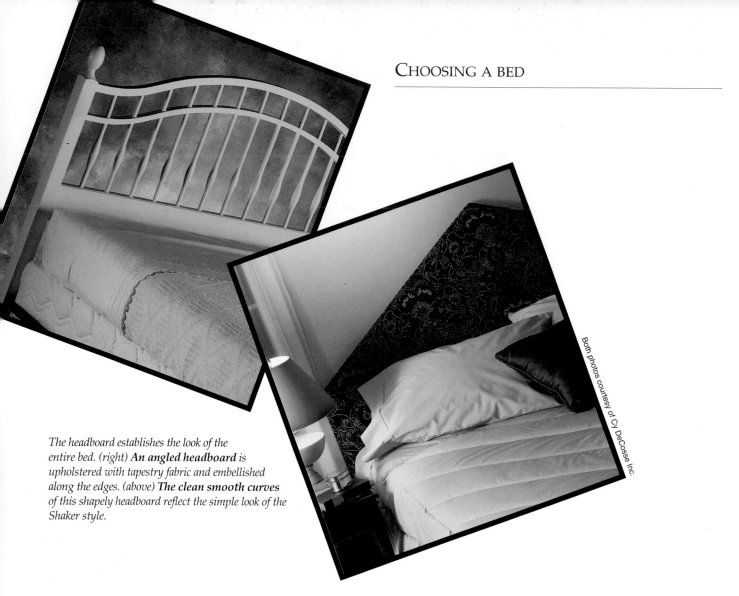

The headboard establishes the look of the entire bed. (right) **An angled headboard** *is upholstered with tapestry fabric and embellished along the edges. (above)* **The clean smooth curves** *of this shapely headboard reflect the simple look of the Shaker style.*

Both photos courtesy of Cy DeCosse Inc.

The traditional American bed has a standard steel frame and usually comes without a headboard. Bed frames come as separate pieces; the headboard, footboard and side rails are assembled to form one unit. Today, many bed frame styles, such as the look of traditional brass bed frames, are reproduced in lacquered wood.

The headboard is the element that dictates the decorative style of a bed. Rattan or wicker headboards have a casual, contemporary feel, while headboards made of fine woods, such as mahogany or walnut, create a more traditional look. Padded or upholstered headboards have a soft appeal. The ideal headboard is functional as well as attractive. For example, headboards with built-in storage are ideal options for bedrooms with limited space.

The four-poster bed frame creates a traditional quality in a bedroom, while cozy canopy beds create the feeling of a room within a room. Canopy and four-poster beds require high ceilings and a large space, or they can easily overwhelm a room. Platform beds are raised one or more steps off the floor and often feature some kind of storage space built into the frame. These beds require no box spring because the mattress sits directly on the platform. Futons and waterbeds require special frames suited to their specific mattresses.

Futon bed frames are usually made of wide wooden slats attached to a simple frame. The slats are spaced closely enough to keep the futon from sagging, and far enough apart to allow air to circulate around the mattress. Many futon bases double as sofa platforms as well.

Waterbed design has evolved dramatically since its introduction in the 1960s. For these beds, a good-quality frame plays an important role in the support of the waterbed. It is not so much the weight of the bed that is a concern—waterbeds weigh about as much as a refrigerator —it is the stress on the sides of the frame.

An expansive four-poster bed fills this bedroom with traditional flavor. Beds such as canopies and four-posters need lots of room, both overhead and on the sides.

Back to basics. *The natural theme of this bedroom goes so far as to use actual tree branches in the bed frame.*

A delightful daybed *doubles as a sitting bench or sofa. Matching material was used to create a swag that drapes loosely over the bed and frames this fancy setting.*

(left) **A mattress becomes a bed** *by simply backing it with cushions, or raising it on a platform or base.*
(right) **Frequently paired with a bed skirt**, *a duvet cover protects a duvet, or comforter, from wear.*

Photos courtesy of Cy DeCosse Inc.

CHOOSING A BED

When choosing a new mattress, start by evaluating the old one. Do you like the size? How about the support? Also consider the size, and sleeping or lounging habits, of the people who will be using the mattress. A comfortable bed begins with a comfortable, quality mattress and a good foundation, such as a box spring or raised platform.

Basically, there are two types of mattresses; innerspring and foam. Innerspring mattresses come in the same standard sizes as bed frames; king, queen, full (or double) and twin or (single). Innerspring mattresses are composed of springs connected in various ways: open springs, individual springs aligned in rows within the mattress; continuous springs, a network of connected wire instead of individual springs; and pocketed springs, with each spring enclosed in its own pocket. Pocketed springs are considered to be the best.

The comfort of an innerspring mattress is also greatly affected by its wire gauge and spring count. The lower the gauge of the wire, the stronger the coil. The heaviest, or strongest, you'll find is 13, and 21 is the highest, or lightest. To determine whether a mattress has a good coil count, remember that twin mattresses should have more than 200 coils, and larger mattresses

should have at least 300 coils. Also check the quality of the cushioning and insulation that are added. The more layers, the more comfortably you'll sleep.

Foam, futons and waterbeds are alternatives to the traditional innerspring mattress. Consider a foam mattress if you need to fit an odd-size or antique bed. A foam mattress can be easily cut and tailored to fit almost any size or shape of frame. A good-quality foam mattress can be just as comfortable as an innerspring.

Originally from Japan, futons were first made of cotton batting inside a heavy fabric casing. Contemporary futons are essentially the same except they usually have an extra layer of foam or other padding for better durability.

Waterbed mattresses have improved dramatically; they now come with comfortable foam edges or use baffles to control wave motion. A "hard-side" model has a vinyl mattress, liner and heater encased in a frame. A "soft-side" waterbed looks just like an innerspring mattress. Soft-side waterbeds are usually composed of easy-to-fill tubes that sit side by side in an upholstered cover. A polyurethane liner is used to contain the water in case of a leak. Be sure the vinyl is at least 20 millimeters thick to protect the cover against leaks.

An exotic, tropical motif is created by simply adding a natural wicker headboard to a basic bed frame. The theme is enhanced by the ethnic print on the accent pillows.

Mattress and box spring sets may be the bed of choice in our Western world, but in Japan the simple futon is the favorite. An American evolution in futon frames is an adjustable frame that converts from an upright couch structure to a flat bed frame.

Design
SPECIAL FEATURES

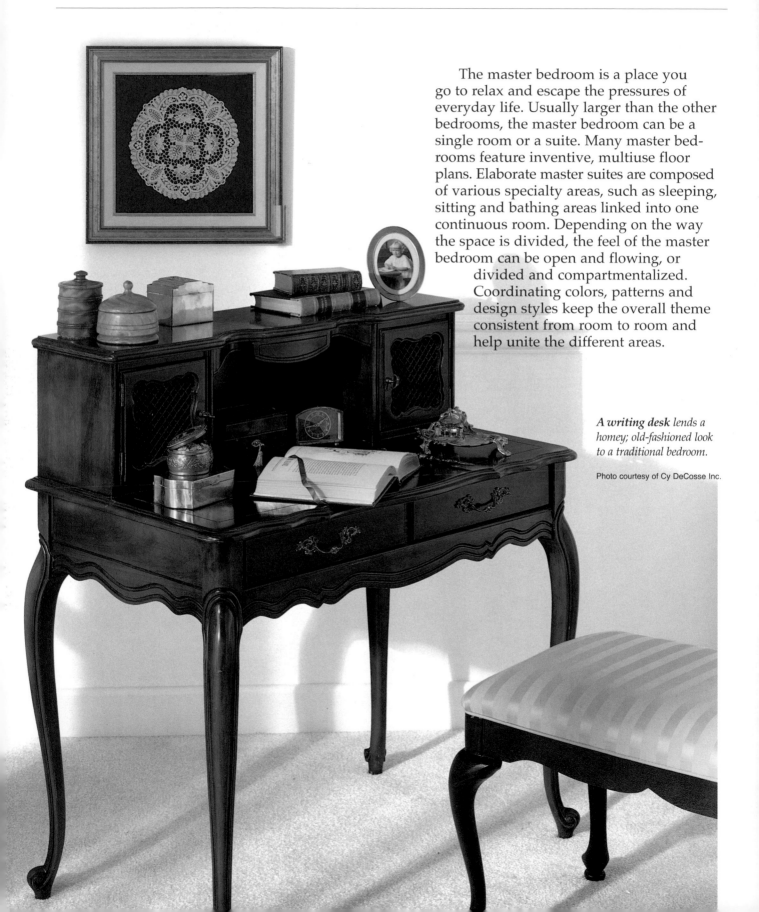

The master bedroom is a place you go to relax and escape the pressures of everyday life. Usually larger than the other bedrooms, the master bedroom can be a single room or a suite. Many master bedrooms feature inventive, multiuse floor plans. Elaborate master suites are composed of various specialty areas, such as sleeping, sitting and bathing areas linked into one continuous room. Depending on the way the space is divided, the feel of the master bedroom can be open and flowing, or divided and compartmentalized. Coordinating colors, patterns and design styles keep the overall theme consistent from room to room and help unite the different areas.

*A **writing desk** lends a homey; old-fashioned look to a traditional bedroom.*

Photo courtesy of Cy DeCosse Inc.

Photo courtesy of Interlubke, North America

Modern modular systems offer a variety of beds, chests, wall panels, shelves and tables that make it simple to achieve the look you truly desire. The many different ways of combining elements offers you total freedom of choice.

(above) **Creating a bedroom sitting area** is as easy as adding a comfortable overstuffed chair to the corner of the bedroom.
(left) **A separate sitting area** is a special feature that expands the versatility and usability of a bedroom.

Bottom photos courtesy of GenCorp

37

The master suite is the ultimate place to pamper yourself. Plan this room so that the modern conveniences that make your life easier are within reach from the comfort of your bed. Possible options include a fireplace or a built-in entertainment center. You can also add a bar, an under-counter refrigerator, even a popcorn machine.

A master bedroom doesn't need to be huge and sprawling; you can create a comfortable master bedroom in an average-size room. Dividing the space is one way; a low divider can subtly define different areas without making the space seem too confining. Knocking out a wall can merge two smaller rooms together, creating a large open master bedroom. Windows, skylights and sliding doors are all ways to bring in more light, and make a space seem larger and more open.

Make the most efficient use of spare bedrooms by giving them more than one function. With careful planning, spare bedrooms can also double as dens, sewing rooms, home offices and more. Moveable panels and folding screens are easy ways to provide privacy. A sitting room just off the bedroom, rather than right in it, has the advantage of allowing you to close a door between the two areas. Careful planning and the use of built-ins and modular storage can help make maximum use of the space.

For rooms that are specifically guest rooms, a night table, closet space and night lighting are special ways to make your guests feel at home.

When is a double bed not a double bed? When it is two twin beds that glide together on rails. An exciting option in bedroom furniture design, the rail allows you to push the beds together when you want and apart when you don't. This revolutionary rail system makes it easy to clean under the bed as well.

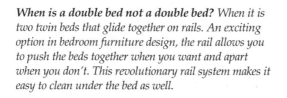

A PORTFOLIO OF

BEDROOM
IDEAS

SELECTING A STYLE

Clean and uncluttered describes the contemporary style that is carried throughout this bedroom. The modern motif is accented by black leather, black lacquer and contemporary chrome tables, specifically designed to fit by the bed.

The personality, or ambience, of a bedroom is created by the feelings it inspires when you enter. This ambience is a matter of personal taste, not a specific style. You can express an overall feeling or ambience within any given style by coordinating furnishings, accessories, colors and materials that express the overall feeling you desire for your bedroom. For instance, if country is a style that appeals to you, you can create a bedroom that has a casual country feel by using simple, rustic furnishings. If a softer look is what you want, create a romantic country bedroom that features gingham and lace, and lots of ruffles. Most interior design motifs are influenced by a classic style, such as stately traditional, casual country, sleek and simple contemporary or an eclectic mix of styles.

(left) **The decorative design** style of the old-fashioned iron bed frame, combined with the Mission-style design of the bed stand and dresser, reflect the strong influence of early American style.

(bottom left) **A carefully coordinated kid's space** is designed to stay in style well into the teen years. A colorful border, located midway up the wall, introduces a clever sports theme to the design scheme.

(bottom right) **Traditional influences,** such as the decorative brass curtain rod and tiebacks, are also reflected in the intricately carved trunk and other elements in this Victorian-style bedroom.

Photos this page courtesy of GenCorp

Photos both pages courtesy of Broyhill

PERIOD STYLES

(above) **A hint of Chippendale** *style influences the classic design of this Federal-style bed frame and mirror. The mahogany frame features elaborate rope-carved detailing fancied during the Federal period.*

Period styles reflect the design motifs that were created at various periods in history. They are usually a reflection of the social and economic trends popular at that time. Certain colors are associated with particular period styles. Colonial and Federal periods are rich with deep, dark reds, greens and blues. The English periods include the graceful 18th-century Georgian period, which produced the furniture styles of the great cabinetry makers of the era: Adam, Chippendale, Hepplewhite, and Sheraton. This period also featured colors with rich hues and scenic wallpapers.

The American Federal period was inspired by the neoclassical revival. Walls were painted plaster or covered with formal papers from Europe and Asia. Symbols of the eagle and other classic American revolutionary symbols were prevalent. The best-known example of the Federal style is Thomas Jefferson's home, Monticello.

Colonial style recreates the look of nineteenth-century European colonial experience, when the early settlers had to make do with furnishings that were primitive, imported or both. The popular Colonial Revival in the late 19th century created what many people today think of as Colonial style: a mixture of American Country with its painted wood paneling and stenciled folk art, Boston rocking chairs and Windsor chairs of early Federal style.

French period styles include elaborate scrollwork and decoration. Neoclassical Louis XVI furniture featured straight lines and geometric motifs.

Tall, tapering bedposts *are a common design detail found during the Federal period. This open-top bed design evolved from the ancient boxed-in bedsteads of Elizabethan times.*

The Victorian period includes a great diversity of styles. The look we generally think of as Victorian is a mixture of many characteristics.

During that period, known as the "Industrial Age," people were surrounded by such inventions as proper plumbing, the motor car and the first electric lift. Designers were able to take advantage of an incredible range of new chemical dyes. The styles reflected the prosperity of the time. Interior design motifs ranged from the elegant lines of the early Victorian interiors with light greens, lilacs and yellows, to the mid-Victorian period, characterized by overstuffed furniture and richly colored dark rooms. Victorian style also includes needlework rugs, floral prints and patterns, elaborate window treatments and grandfather clocks.

Victorian furniture, in all the different styles of the period, is still relatively cheap—one reason this design style remains popular throughout the world.

Photo courtesy of Cy DeCosse Inc.

Elements of Early American furniture styles can be seen in the four-poster mahogany bed. The tall, tapering bedposts and the mixture of distinctive colors are the details that set the tone for this setting.

Photo courtesy of GenCorp

(above) Elaborate elegance is everywhere in this gentle Victorian-style setting. A decorative swag, in a coordinated print, drapes around the back of the daybed and flows freely over the sides.

(right) A classic four-poster bed frame, with a delicate lace canopy, creates a bedroom setting that has a very Victorian influence.

Early American influences *can be seen in the furniture of this bedroom setting. These furniture designs, now considered traditional, evolved from earlier periods and styles of designers such as Georgian or Hepplewhite. Rich wood tones and large exposed overhead beams enhance the rustic flavor.*

Photo courtesy of Laura Ashley

(left) **The distinctive round shape** and detailed carving on the antique-looking commode are representative of early American furniture makers. These early designers established their own cabinetry style, which incorporated traditional and neoclassic elements.

(below) **Simple, straight lines** in the dresser and bed frame represent the utilitarian design style, popular during the Federal period, referred to as Shaker. Round wooden boxes, known as "Shaker boxes," add an interesting accent.

Photo courtesy of GenCorp

(above) **Influences of the French Provincial** *style are seen in the flowery pastel prints of the wallpaper and window treatments, as well as in the intricate design details of the dressing table and mirror.*

(right) **Carefully coordinated bedding** *and wallcovering components create the perfect background to showcase furniture styles from the American Federal period.*

Photos both pages courtesy of GenCorp

Photos both pages courtesy of GenCorp

TRADITIONAL

(above) *An antique, rope-turned bed frame is covered with a homemade, hand-stitched quilt, creating a cozy corner with a touch of both traditional and country influences.*

Traditional is a decorating term that describes the general characteristics of the period styles. Traditional implies certain design influences that can be seen in the graceful shapes and stylings of classic furniture designers such as Chippendale or Sheraton. Traditional decorating schemes are not exact re-creations of period styles, but are combinations of an individual's favorite motifs, colors and patterns from different periods. Lavish and detailed, traditional bedrooms feature rich woods and patterned fabrics in distinctive colors.

Traditional bedrooms are cozy and comfortable, often decorated with a mix of patterns on walls, windows and beds. These bedrooms are the perfect place to express your own personal taste with favorite antiques, family photos and collections of personal memorabilia.

Traditional bedrooms are lavishly decorated with various fabrics, from elaborate tapestries to sateen, with long draperies that flow luxuriously onto the floor. The bed is often dressed with layers of bedspreads and bed skirts. Furniture of rich mahogany or cherry, with intricate details, is common in traditional rooms, as are brass lamps, bishop sleeve curtains, ruffled pillow shams and four-poster beds.

The smooth design style of a traditional sleigh bed is dressed with a combination of patterned sheets and pillow covers. A Windsor-style chair with a bentwood back, a rag rug and the round Shaker box next to the bed, all denote the traditional flavor of this decor.

English traditional reflects the cold, damp climate and the warmth that is desired in an English home. This warmth is found in English tweed, as well as hunter green, royal blue, crimson and mustard. Warm English colors also include natural browns, grays and creams, as well as the bright colors of garden flowers.

English traditional style includes Victorian cabinetry, Regency furniture in black and gold, Edinburgh or Waterford crystal and Chippendale desks. A traditional English country bedroom is large and spacious.

French traditional has some similarities to English traditional, but the character and flavor is much different. Since the climate of France is warmer and less rainy, French rooms don't focus so much on a central fireplace. Pastels don't work well with the deep, ruddy shades of English traditional, but a French style can be flavored with more subtle shades, such as peach, rose, beige, pale lemon, Wedgwood blue, muted green and rich cream.

*An **intricately carved** four-poster bed establishes a traditional theme in this bedroom decorating scheme. The authentic claw-foot table and antique wicker cases spice up this typically traditional setting.*

(above) ***A traditional bedroom*** *isn't complete without including a wooden rocking chair. This Windsor-style rocker features turned spindles and a hand-painted finish.*

(left) ***A simple Shaker-style bed frame*** *was embellished with soft curves and other details to soften the visual appeal. Ruffled curtains, rag dolls and decorative Shaker boxes all enhance this early American bedroom setting.*

Photos both pages courtesy of GenCorp

The materials used in traditional French rooms are more lush and luxurious. There is much more use of fabric than in traditional British decor. French traditional also includes intricately detailed Austrian shades, with lots of molding, trim and borders.

If there is one universal traditional style, it is wicker. In the East and West alike, the internationally known willow is bent and twisted to a desired shape. Wicker furniture can be found in traditional styles as well as modern, country and Oriental.

Soft, subtle pastels, whitewashed furniture and billowy balloon shades represent classic qualities of French traditional style. A unique bed design features a headboard that has the look of a louvered blind.

Photo courtesy of GenCorp

(left) **Straight, boxlike design** and minimal detail in this four-poster bed are characteristics representative of the traditional Mission style. Whitewashed walls and exposed beams in the ceiling enhance the overall feeling.

(below) **The square lines** of this bed frame design were strongly influenced by the Mission style. A gunmetal blue color wash adds a Federal flavor as well.

Photo courtesy of Broyhill

Photo courtesy of Cy DeCosse Inc.

COUNTRY

Colorful gingham and white cotton give this bedroom a comfortable country flavor. A Victorian influence can be seen in the antique iron bed frame and Tiffany table lamp.

American country is characterized by a return to basics—handmade furniture, stenciled walls and antique quilts. Today's contemporary country is simpler and cleaner than ever before, incorporating fewer accessories, larger patterns and lighter wood finishes. Two of the 19th-century furniture styles, Shaker and Mission, work well with contemporary country because of their clean, simple design.

A country-style bedroom should have an overall feeling of comfort and gentleness. Country bedrooms can be romantic, fresh, demure and simple, or they can be crowded with rustic collectables. Victorian and Edwardian iron or brass beds are very effective in country bedrooms. Old stripped, whitewashed or painted dressers and chests say country, as do rag rugs and old patchwork quilts.

American country features simplicity: calico, large rough ceiling beams, porch swings, flower boxes, grandfather clocks, denim and linen. Country colors are muted silvers and pewters, and other natural colors found just out a window. Country yellow is vivid and bright, not creamy or pale. Country greens reflect the countryside; spring green, pine green and apple green. Country blues are like the sky, or deep indigo blue. Country red, a rich apple red, is used sparingly throughout the house.

Ruffled pillow covers, in colorful country patterns and colors, are combined with a hand-crafted quilt to create a delightful dressing for this old-fashioned, iron-framed bed.

American country encompasses many regional styles. To create your own American country motif, combine features you favor from each. One of the universal rules of American country is: function. The glorification of the ordinary object used every day, whether it's a patchwork quilt or an old milk can, is what the look is all about.

American country styles also reflect certain regions, such as Southwestern, which reflects the colors and images that are a part of the Southwestern desert. Walls are more often plain than patterned, and colors range from muted to vibrant hues drawn from the surrounding environment.

The cottage gardens of the British countryside are the inspiration behind the English country look, where floral chintzes are used to cover overstuffed sofas and chairs. French Provincial, the country look of France, is different from that of American, in that it is more simple than rustic. French country features vivid hues and patterns. French Provincial is very different from the French traditional style, in that it reflects the rural look of the French provinces, whereas French traditional expresses the stylings of French cities, such as Paris.

An old-fashioned pie safe becomes a beautiful place to store bedding. The handcrafted quilts are a colorful accent for a look that's completely country.

The vibrant colors and patterns of the American Southwest are reflected in the wallpaper and bedding accessories, as well as the painted iron bed frame.

PORTFOLIO

A lace-covered canopy bed is the centerpiece of this romantic country motif. A handmade quilt, an old-fashioned pitcher and basin set and an antique painted chest enhance the country effect.

The textured, aged look of antique wicker is beautifully complemented by smooth, crisp cotton bedding. A dainty lace valance adds a delicate detail to the country accent of this room.

An antique iron bed is dressed for the country, covered in ginghams and calico, eyelet and lace bedding.

63

INTERNATIONAL

The fresh clean look *of the whitewashed Mission-style furniture becomes part of an international mix that includes French Provincial and early American styles. A Scandinavian influence can also be detected in the decorative iron sculptures displayed throughout the room.*

Influences of English, Italian, Japanese, Spanish, French, Scandinavian and Oriental styles are all reflected in the international style of interior design. These influences can be described even more specifically in terms such as American Country, French Provincial, English Country or American Southwest.

Neoclassic was the first real international style. This design style re-creates the art and architecture of ancient Greece, Rome and early Egypt, as it was expressed in Italy and other European countries years later. As with Victorian, neoclassic includes a variety of more specific styles, created because different countries adapted this style to suit their own tastes and requirements.

Scandinavian influence on an international motif can be achieved by including pieces reflective of King Gustav III and his passion for French Louis XVI styling. During his reign, a new, lighter, less formal design style replaced the heavy formal look. This light, whimsical style is referred to as Gustavian and is the most representative of what is commonly recognized as the Scandinavian style. Influenced by the colors of the northern lights, international design motifs that feature the Scandinavian style incorporate neutral blond woods and make liberal use of white, blue and gray, as well as furniture that has been whitewashed, pickled or color washed, or given a coat of a translucent, pastel color.

Out of Africa. *Interesting artifacts from African travels are prominently displayed throughout this bedroom, giving it an international appeal. Wicker furniture adds the flavor of the Philippines, and the stained glass that frames the large window brings a European quality to the setting.*

65

The style that has the most formal influence on international settings is Oriental. The art and accessories that form this style add a romantic, exotic accent to traditional or contemporary settings. The influences of the Orient include grass mats, rice paper, cane, rattan, bamboo, teak and wicker. It also includes delicate things that are portable, such as paper and silk screens painted with intricate and realistic landscapes and framed with carved rosewood. In Oriental design, every object has a purpose. Beautiful and portable are attributes of the Oriental style that embrace anything that is lightweight, translucent and foldable.

The simple beauty of the Oriental look allows this style to mix easily with many motifs. Although the Orient has some of the oldest cultures, Oriental furnishings remain modern in feeling because of their understated attention to details and great adaptability.

__The ornate style__ of this bed frame reflects the look and feel of the Far East. The soft pastel purples, yellows and greens, evocative of the French Provincial style, provide a beautiful backdrop for the mix of international influences in this bedroom.

Photo courtesy of Broyhill

The lavish look of a French Provincial-style sleigh bed is combined with the simple style of the American Mission influence. Combining these ethnic influences creates a beautiful blend of international flavor.

This romantic bedroom was internationally inspired. Strongly influenced by the French Provincial style, this bedroom features a sleigh bed and armoire that reflect the stylings of Louis XV. The delicate demeanor of antique wicker lightens the look of the setting and influences the room with a tropical or southern plantation appeal.

Photos this page courtesy of Grange

The influence of American Mission style can be seen in the refined look of this French Provincial bedroom. The sleigh bed, Mission-style wardrobe and bedside table are examples of the simple, comfortable charm that exemplifies this style.

Photo courtesy of Grange

The colors that evoke the influence of an Oriental style include jade green, deep reds, brilliant yellows, vivid purples and oranges, and deep tropical fuchsias. Always an indication of an Oriental influence is the use of a lot of black. "High Style" Oriental is the lavish style from the Oriental Empire period. The influence of this Oriental style can be seen in a setting that features a high style screen as an object of art. International settings that are influenced by this high style Oriental look exhibit the fabulous wealth of the Orient in silk, jade, ebony, porcelain, inlay and carvings.

After its introduction to England in the early seventeenth century, the neoclassic style became widely popular. Today a variety of styles reflect the neoclassical taste for stripes, vaulted ceilings and military symbols such as crossed swords, spears, arrows and shield-back chairs. Other features taken directly from neoclassic architecture include Greek-key borders, lyre-backed chairs, pilasters and columns, taken from classical Greek designs.

Rich colors and textures that adorn this iron daybed can be attributed to the influences of the Far East. The jade green in the marble table adds an elegant Oriental appeal. The translucent natural fiber shades give the room an open, airy feeling and a finished look that has a strong international appeal.

Also considered neoclassical are Egyptian elements such as sphinxes, lions' paws, scroll-back chairs and sofas. These elements are complemented by muslin draperies, elaborate window treatments and fabric trims, marble and lavish use of ebony, gilt, black and white.

Photos both pages courtesy of Pier One Imports

(two photos above) **A visit to Jamaica** *or the South Pacific inspired this interior style. Wicker, with an antique white finish, brings a taste of the tropics to this bright, breezy bedroom.*

The international influence *of Africa and the Middle East can be seen in the distinctive patterns and colors used throughout the room. Natural fiber rugs and a muslin bedspread combine with the wicker furniture and accessories to add textural interest to this natural, neutral-colored decor.*

Photo courtesy of Broyhill

Photo courtesy of Cy DeCosse, Inc

ECLECTIC

(above) **Neoclassic and contemporary styles,** *with a touch of traditional American Shaker in the bed frame, are nicely tied together by a soothing, dusty rose monochromatic background.*

Mixing the styles of different periods and regions creates an eclectic style. This look is similar to the effect you achieve when you blend traditional and contemporary elements for a transitional look. Eclectic decorating relies on the art of integrating elements from all styles. An example of a successful eclectic setting is one that provides the warmth of traditional with the simplicity of contemporary.

One way to successfully combine a variety of styles is to carry a repeating color or pattern throughout the room. Continuity is the key to an integrated and sophisticated eclectic look. Another way to achieve an eclectic effect is to decide on the ambience you want—formal or informal—and maintain that mood as you decorate.

Exciting and more personal decors are often achieved by blending styles, rather than following one theme. A mix of contemporary and traditional furniture can offer an effective contrast. To help balance the look, pieces of furniture should be similar in weight and proportion.

Exciting and more personal decors are achieved by blending styles rather than strictly following one theme. A mix of contemporary and traditional furniture can offer an effective contrast.

73

Often, contemporary pieces of furniture are inspired by familiar traditional styles, making them ideally suitable for eclectic decorating.

Color can be used to unify varied styles of furnishings so they work together. Repeat only a few of the colors and fabrics in the room, and avoid mixing several patterns.

If you like to decorate your home in a way that is uniquely yours, you can also look to the rare finds that can be found at antique stores, salvage yards and flea markets. Using secondhand finds can help you assemble an eclectic mix that adds just the right personality and style to a bedroom.

An assortment of garage sale odds and ends brings out an elegant, old-world look that would work in any eclectic setting.

Collectibles, like this brass elephant and these antique books, can be showcased on table lamps. The lamps are easily assembled using figurine arms and other basic lamp parts.

Inspired by Old World influences, *this traditional sleigh bed setting borrows from many classic influences, as seen in the gilded finish on the bedside table and in the antique Persian rug.*

Photos both pages courtesy of Cy DeCosse Inc.

(top) ***A vintage kimono*** *is hung on a dowel, creating a simple, yet dramatic, wall display. The authentic style of the kimono is artfully displayed above a collection of art deco-style bottles and a contemporary table lamp for an exciting eclectic mix.*

(right) ***Embroidered tablecloth****, with a casual country appeal, is swagged elegantly over the refined look of lace curtains. Raffia and nosegay of preserved and silk floral materials are used as embellishments in this eclectic window embellishment.*

(opposite page) ***A simple space*** *is styled with a minimal assortment of eclectic accents. The decor of this multifunctional room needs to be neutral enough to work in a social or bedroom setting.*

(right) **Smooth lines** *and soothing monotone colors keep the look simple and smart. An eclectic combination of Shaker boxes and a Scandinavian-style, high-back chair reflect the same graceful design used in the bed frame.*

(below) **Armoires** *may be colorfully painted and lined with wallcovering, to neatly finish the interior. They are an ideal place to house an artfully arranged eclectic display.*

Photo courtesy of Bruce Hardwood Floors

Photo courtesy of Interlubke, North America

CONTEMPORARY

Contemporary style encompasses a variety of different design elements, from the Art Deco style of the late 1920s, to the brightly colored modern Italian furnishings. To many, contemporary means the clean, unadorned lines and bare woods representative of the Scandinavian style.

Contemporary interior design evokes a style that's simple and strong, often described as high tech, or minimalist. Furniture is designed more for form than decoration; brass, glass, chrome and steel are often incorporated into the design scheme. Open rooms, free of clutter, with abundant light and minimal furnishings, contribute to a sense of spaciousness that is associated with contemporary style.

Contemporary includes the sleek lines and warm wood of Scandinavian pieces, as well as the Art Nouveau and Bauhaus styles. Contemporary color is usually plain and neutral; when patterns do appear, they are generally abstract or geometric.

(above) **Designed for day,** *as well as night, this chic contemporary bedroom is functional as well as beautiful. The pieces of the chest and wardrobe system link together to form one continuous whole. And the bed includes a relaxing, ergonomically shaped headboard.*

(left) **The sun, the moon and the stars** *are all out in this contemporary setting. Coordinated bedding, with a unique astronomy design, provides a contemporary feel that is carried throughout.*

This dreamy bedroom design is filled with wide-awake new ideas that are not only beautiful, but functional as well. A softly upholstered headboard is also an ergonomically shaped backrest that provides perfect back support for reading or enjoying breakfast in bed.

Sleek Eurostyle design has an ultracontemporary feel with elements that focus on simple, functional details. Art Deco is another contemporary design style that includes such design details as rare woods, delicate carvings, marquetry and tables of marble inlaid with gilt.

Decorating in a contemporary style means keeping the number of furnishings and accessories to a minimum. Color is also used sparingly. To maintain a spacious, open look, light, cool colors are often used except in large rooms. Elements of a contemporary bedroom include: table lamps of brass or chrome, with sleek design lines; polished metals that add richness to the decor; and

lacquered furniture that has a slick, polished appearance. Contemporary end tables and dressers often do not have visible drawer pulls.

Berber carpeting or highly polished hardwood floors work well in a contemporary bedroom. Window treatments are chosen for privacy and simplicity in styling. Tailored blinds or pleated shades are good choices for contemporary window treatments.

Dramatic lighting is an effective way to enhance the refined look of a contemporary setting. Recessed lighting, cove lighting and ceiling-mounted track lights are all effective choices for a contemporary bedroom setting.

Let there be light. *In this contemporary setting, clothes are stored away in tall wardrobes with open units that could house a variety of items. A futuristic-looking vase holder is suspended over the bed as an interesting accent. Other creative comforts in this space include a glass-topped side*

(left) **The bedside table,** *from the bedroom above, swings up and over the bed and is adjustable to any position you desire.*

Photos both pages courtesy of Interlubke, North America

Contemporary new designs are integrated with the latest designs in built-in arrangements. Numerous sofas and chairs that convert into beds are also available to help make the most economical use of space. Contemporary furniture designs include new configurations for modular chairs and sleep sofa units that can be pushed together or unfolded to form a bed.

Other types of bed frames, such as those used for futons, assimilate easily into a contemporary setting. The functional futon can be rolled up or folded to form a casual couch, or you can buy sliding frames that transform a couch into a bed.

(all photos)
Perfect for studio apartments *or spare rooms that perform double duty. This contemporary bedroom works even within the confines of a steeply sloping ceiling. The arrangement of chests and shelves holds the hidden asset of a double bed. By day, it functions as a cabinet, with plenty of storage space; by night, it becomes a bed that quickly folds out and back as the need arises.*

Thinking ahead. *A well-planned youth room bridges the gap between childhood and teen years. The furniture system is flexible—not too babyish, and not too grown-up. The spacious floor plan leaves lots of room for activities.*

Photo courtesy of Broyhill

Photo courtesy of GenCorp

YOUTH ROOMS

Personality, durability and adaptability are key when designing bedrooms for children and teens. These bedrooms should be an expression of the child's identity and a comfortable haven where they can play, read, study or just relax.

Choose durable, washable flooring, carpeting and wallcoverings for a child's bedroom, because wear and tear are inevitable. Furniture, fabrics and surfaces that hold up to finger paints and crayons should be incorporated as much as possible.

Furniture in a child's room should be sturdy and stable, with no sharp edges or protruding hooks. Always use lead-free paint on furniture and any other painted surface in a child's bedroom.

Bats, balls, bright colors and wallpaper with a baseball card border make this fun-filled bedroom a super setting for any slugger.

(top left) **Finger painting at its finest.** *This fanciful border suggests fun and creative freedom, the ideal setting for an aspiring artist.*

(top right) **Complete with a castle,** *this kid's space could even cure Humpty Dumpty. A large activity area provides plenty of room for play, while a bookcase with big open shelves stores everything from stuffed bunnies to baseballs.*

(below) **A decorative screen,** *made out of fabric, adds interest and provides a special play area. The hot air balloons are cutouts from a companion wallcovering.*

Trucks, trucks, and more trucks; *what could say more about this child's interests? Fun decor and big bold print feature primary colors for the primary years.*

Farmyard friends *have come for a visit. A child's table and chair set are just the right size to comfortably accommodate a child in this cozy play corner.*

Because kids are constantly changing, the type of bedroom they desire will also be changing. Think ahead when designing for kids: Will the design be easy to modify in five years, or even two? Is there room for storage, studying, a doll collection, or just plain roughhousing? Sufficient space for all these activities makes the space truly multifunctional.

Teddy bears and puppy dogs *are there to say good night and sleep tight, when the child whose room this is goes to bed for the night.*

An attic *has been converted to an upstairs bedroom that's typically for a teenager. The look is complete with designer makeup mirror and a kicky-colored telephone.*

90

Coordinated wallpaper, *with matching bedding accessories, features bright yellow daisies and giant gingham checks. The bright colors and large patterns create a child's space that comes straight from a storybook setting.*

(above) **Higher learning** is emphasized in this corner. Wallpaper with a Mach I border is combined with matching military planes and striped motif. This corner counter creates space for the computer, and built-in drawers add extra storage underneath.

(right) **Polka dots and purples** play a major role in the decor of this active adolescent's bedroom. The busy mixture of bright colors and strong design elements makes a room that's "messy" by design.

Photos both pages courtesy of GenCorp

(right) **Farmyard friends** are all around in this fun-filled room. A sunny spot by the window makes a great play area, complete with a comfortable chair where kids can cuddle close for a bedtime story.

(below) **Colorful rag baskets** are simple and soft, and come in many sizes, from tabletop baskets to large floor baskets that can be used to store items such as stuffed bears, books and building blocks.

LIST OF CONTRIBUTORS

We'd like to thank the following companies for providing the photographs used in this book:

Amtico International, Inc.
6480 Roswell Road
Atlanta, GA 30328
1-800-268-4260

Broyhill Furniture Industries, Inc.
One Broyhill Park
Lenoir, NC 28633
704-758-3111

Bruce Hardwood Floors
A Division of Triangle Pacific Corp.
16803 Dallas Parkway
Dallas, TX 75428
800-526-0308

Casella Lighting
111 Rhode Island
San Francisco, CA 94103
415-626-9600

Conrad Imports
575 Tenth Street
San Francisco, CA 94103-4829
415-626-3303

Country Curtains
Main Street, Dept. 6415
Stockbridge, MA 01262
1-800-456-0321

Crestline Windows & Doors
SNE Corporation
One Wausau Center
Wausau, WI 54402-8007
715-845-1161

GenCorp. Wallcovering Division
Three University Plaza
Hackensack, NJ 07601
201-489-0100

Grange
200 Lexington Avenue
New York, NY 10016
1-800-GRANGE-1

Interlubke
P.O. Box 139
Athens, NY 12015
518-945-1007

Laura Ashley
1-800-367-2000

Pier 1 Imports
301 Commerce Street - Suite 600
Fort Worth, TX 76161-0020
817-878-7660
For the Pier 1 store near you
call 1-800-447-4371